My First Ibibio Dictionary

Colour and Learn Ibibio

kasahorow

2021-09-25
© 2012
KWID: P-KKK10-IBB-EN-2021-09-25

Maame Fosua

Contents

Nwed [Book]

nwed mmi
ikọ mmi
nwed ikọ mmi

...

my book
my word
my word book

Ekpuk [Family]

ekpuk mmi

...

my family

~~~

owowan

/-o-w-o-w-a-n/

woman

ete

/-e-t-e/

man

nsek ayen

/-n-s-e-k -th-e-n/

baby

nne odo

/-n-n-e -o-b-e/

girl

awoden

/-a-w-o-d-e-n/

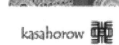

KASAHOROW

boy

Ufɔk [House]

ufɔk mmi

...

my house

~~~

udọk

/-u-dọ-k/

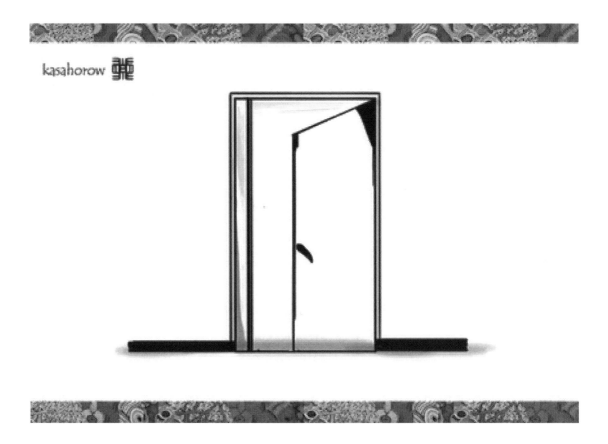

door

windo

/-w-i-n-be/

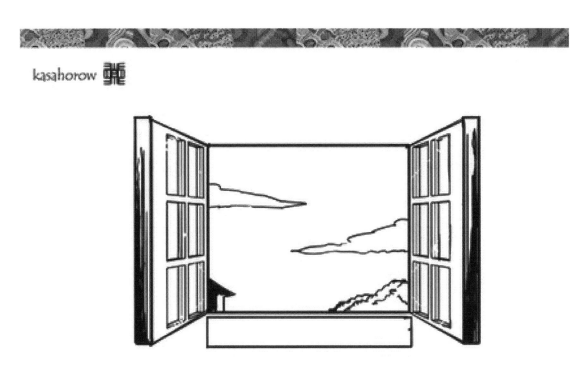

kasahorow

window

atedefon

/-a-t-e-d-e-f-o-n/

kasahorow

telephone

akeme ndise

/-a-k-e-m-e -n-ca-m-e-s-e/

kasahorow

television

mkpo nna

/-m-k-p-o -n-n-a/

kasahorow

bed

Ekpanidim [Shower]

ekpanidim mmi

...

my shower

~~~

eto usuk inua

/-e-t-o -u-s-u-k -i-n-u-a/

kasahorow

toothbrush

mfubo

/-m-f-u-b-o/

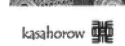

sponge

ofong usuk idem

/-o-f-o-n-g -u-s-u-k -i-d-e-m/

kasahorow

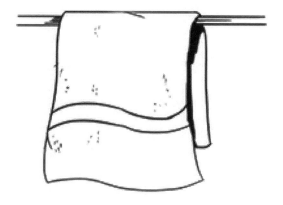

towel

otong

/-o-t-o-n-g/

kasahorow

soap

ukid iso

/-u-k-i-d -i-s-o/

mirror

Ubed [Room]

ubed mmi

...

my room

~~~

afong

/-a-f-o-n-g/

kasahorow

clothes

ikpaukot

/-i-k-p-a-u-k-o-t/

kasahorow

shoe

nkanika

/-n-k-a-n-i-k-a/

kasahorow

clock

akeme iko

/-a-k-e-m-e -i-k-o/

kasahorow

computer

akeme utang iko

/-a-k-e-m-e -u-t-a-n-g -i-k-o/

kasahorow

radio

Ndidia [Food]

ndidia mmi

...

my food

~~~

mboro

/-m-b-o-r-o/

kasahorow

banana

pawpaw

/-p-a-w-p-a-w/

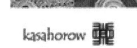

pawpaw

uyo

/-u-y-o/

kasahorow

bread

nserunen

/-n-s-e-r-u-n-e-n/

kasahorow

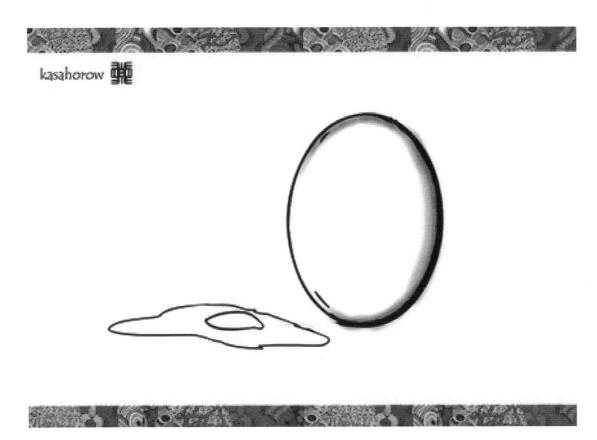

egg

Owo [Body]

owo mmi

...

my body

~~~

ayen

/-th-e-n/

kasahorow

eye

utong

/-u-t-o-n-g/

kasahorow

ear

ibuo

/-i-b-u-o/

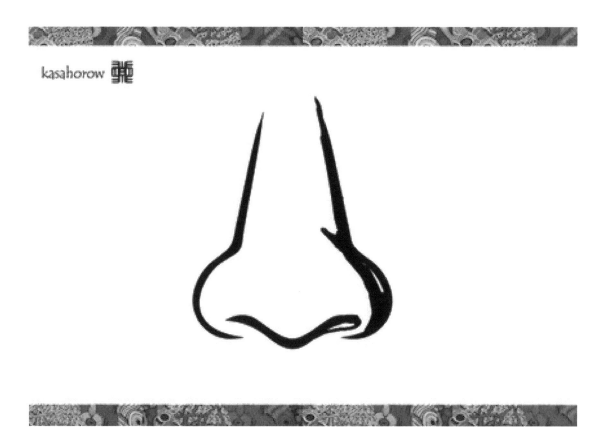

nose

inua

/-i-n-u-a/

kasahorow

mouth

afara

/-a-f-a-r-a/

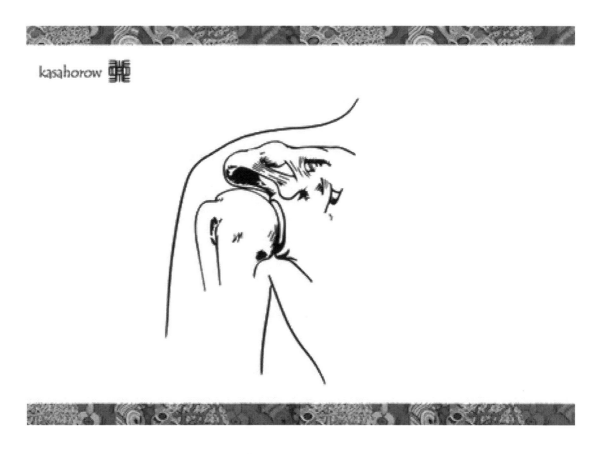

shoulder

ubok

/-u-b-o-k/

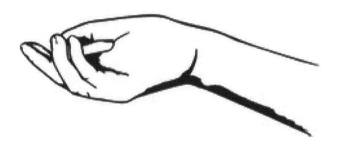

hand

ukot

/-u-k-o-t/

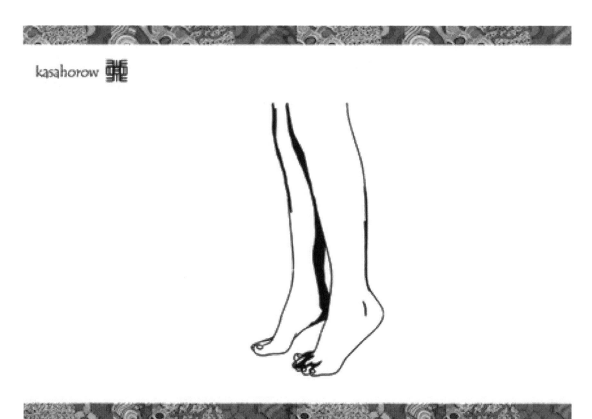

kasahorow

leg

Mme Unam [Pet]

mme unam mmi

...

my pet

~~~

ewa

/-e-w-a/

kasahorow

dog

awa

/-a-w-a/

kasahorow

pussy

iyak

/-i-y-a-k/

kasahorow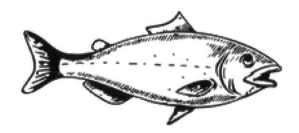

fish

ekpu mbakara

/-e-k-p-u -m-b-a-k-a-r-a/

kasahorow

rabbit

inim

/-i-n-i-m/

kasahorow

parrot

Unam Inwang [Farm Animal]

unam inwang mmi

...

my farm animal

~~~

unen

/-u-n-e-n/

kasahorow

chicken

unen abeke

/-u-n-e-n -a-b-e-k-e/

kasahorow

duck

ebot

/-e-b-o-t/

kasahorow

goat

edong

/-e-b-e-n-g/

sheep

Unam Akai [Forest Animal]

unam akai mmi

...

my forest animal

~~~

utai

/-u-t-a-i/

kasahorow

crocodile

ekpe

/-e-k-p-e/

kasahorow

lion

unam ikot

/-u-n-a-m -i-k-o-t/

kasahorow

zebra

enin

/-e-n-i-n/

kasahorow

elephant

Inwang [Garden]

inwang mmi

...

my garden

~~~

uyai mfang

/-u-y-a-i -m-f-a-n-g/

kasahorow

flower

nkormutu

/-n-k-o-r-m-u-t-u/

kasahorow

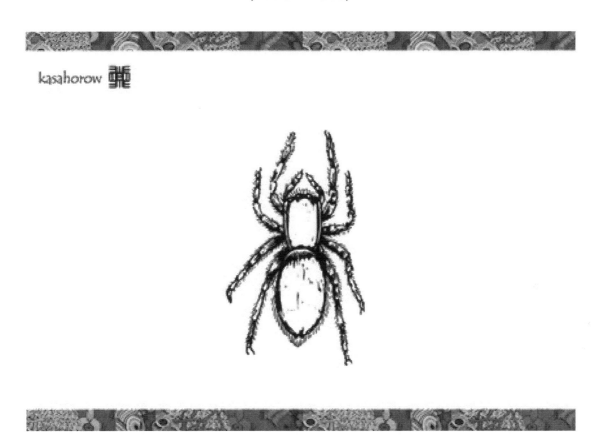

spider

akpa-isong

/-a-k-p-a-i-s-o-n-g/

kasahorow

ant

utong

/-u-t-o-n-g/

kasahorow

worm

akpok

/-a-k-p-o-k/

lizard

Ererimbot [World]

ererimbot mmi

...

my world

~~~

obot

/-o-b-o-t/

mountain

ikpa ayong

/-i-k-p-a -a-y-o-n-g/

kasahorow

cloud

offiong

/-o-f-f-i-o-n-g/

moon

eyo

/-e-y-o/

sun

nta nta offiong

/-n-t-a -n-t-a -o-f-f-i-o-n-g/

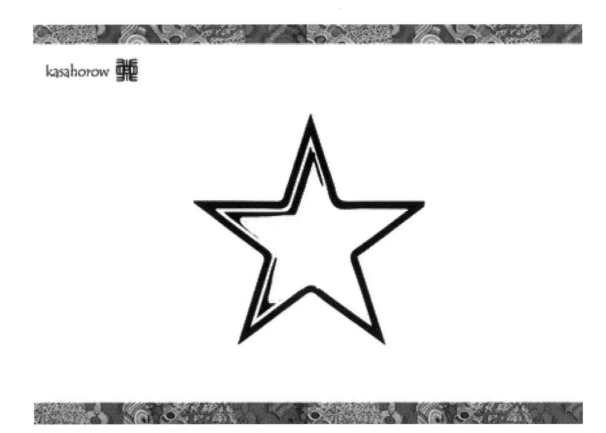

kasahorow

star

Mkpo Isang [Vehicle]

mkpo isang mmi

...

my vehicle

~~~

enang-ukwak

/-e-n-a-n-g-u-k-w-a-k/

kasahorow

bicycle

mkpo isang

/-m-k-p-o -i-s-a-n-g/

kasahorow

car

ubom

/-u-b-o-m/

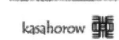

boat

ubom ónyóng

/-u-b-o-m ó-n-yó-n-g/

kasahorow

aeroplane

Ufok Nwed [School]

ufok nwed mmi

...

my school

~~~

akpem nwed

/-a-k-p-e-m -n-w-e-d/

teacher

nkanika

/-n-k-a-n-i-k-a/

kasahorow

bell

nwed

/-n-w-e-d/

kasahorow

book

eto nwed

/-e-t-o -n-w-e-d/

kasahorow

pencil

ekpat

/-e-k-p-a-t/

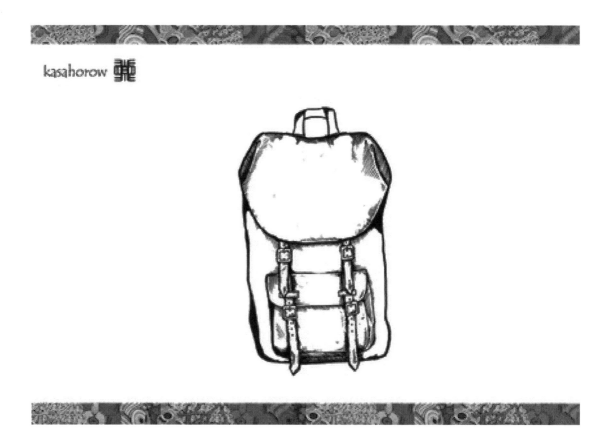

kasahorow

bag

Obio [City]

obio mmi

...

my city

~~~

itie utom

/-i-t-i-e -u-t-o-m/

kasahorow

office

itie udia uwem

/-i-t-i-e -u-ca-m-e-a -u-w-e-m/

kasahorow

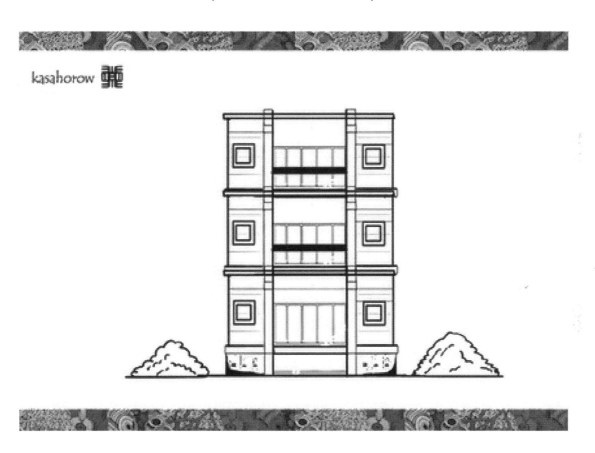

hotel

stadium

/-s-t-a-ca-me-u-m/

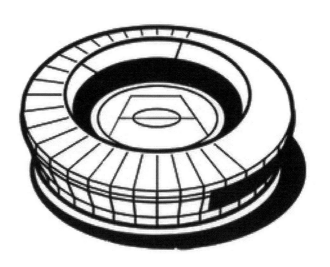

stadium

ntie udua

/-n-t-i-e -u-d-u-a/

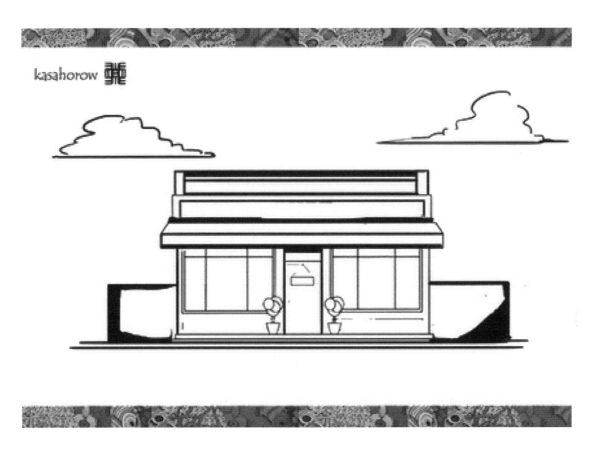

shop

Index

Ibibio kasahorow

ibb.kasahorow.org/app/l

- Count in Ibibio

KWID: P-KKK10-IBB-EN-2021-09-25
www.kasahorow.org/booktalk
Sosongo! Thank you!

Made in the USA
Monee, IL
03 March 2022

92191160R00055